ISBN-13: 978-1542732796

Peggy Louise Parrish
Parma, Idaho
Printed in the United States of America

Welcome to a wonderful adventure with the Letter "F"

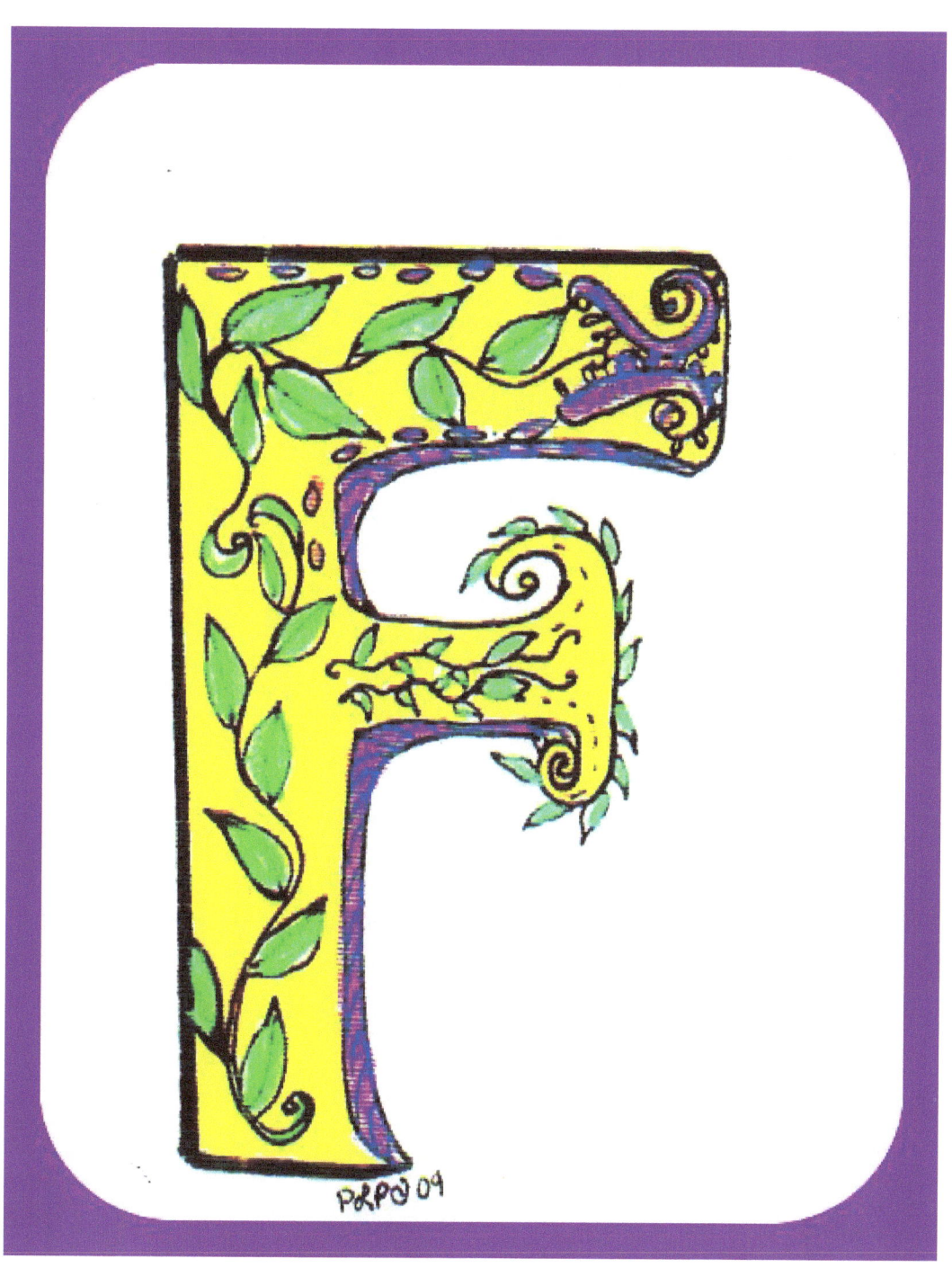

Welcome to a gallery of creative F letters. They are ready and waiting for you to color. You can use any color medium you enjoy. If markers, paint or watercolor pencils are used make sure you place an extra paper behind your work in case color bleeds through. Usually the favorite way to color these is with high quality colored pencils.

The artist's colorized Gallery gives some examples of how you might color them. Feel free to make your own color choices if that's more fun for you.

All these F letters were hand designed by artist Peggy Louise Parrish. If you want to make a few "in house" copies to color different ways you may. Also you can make copies of how you colored them. Maybe you would like to make a friend a card with one of these designs. You must however keep the initials PLP at the bottom of each page. Maybe you will gain some new ideas to make your own style of the Letter F.

The Fancy Letter F
Coloring Book

By Peggy Louise Parrish
c. 2017

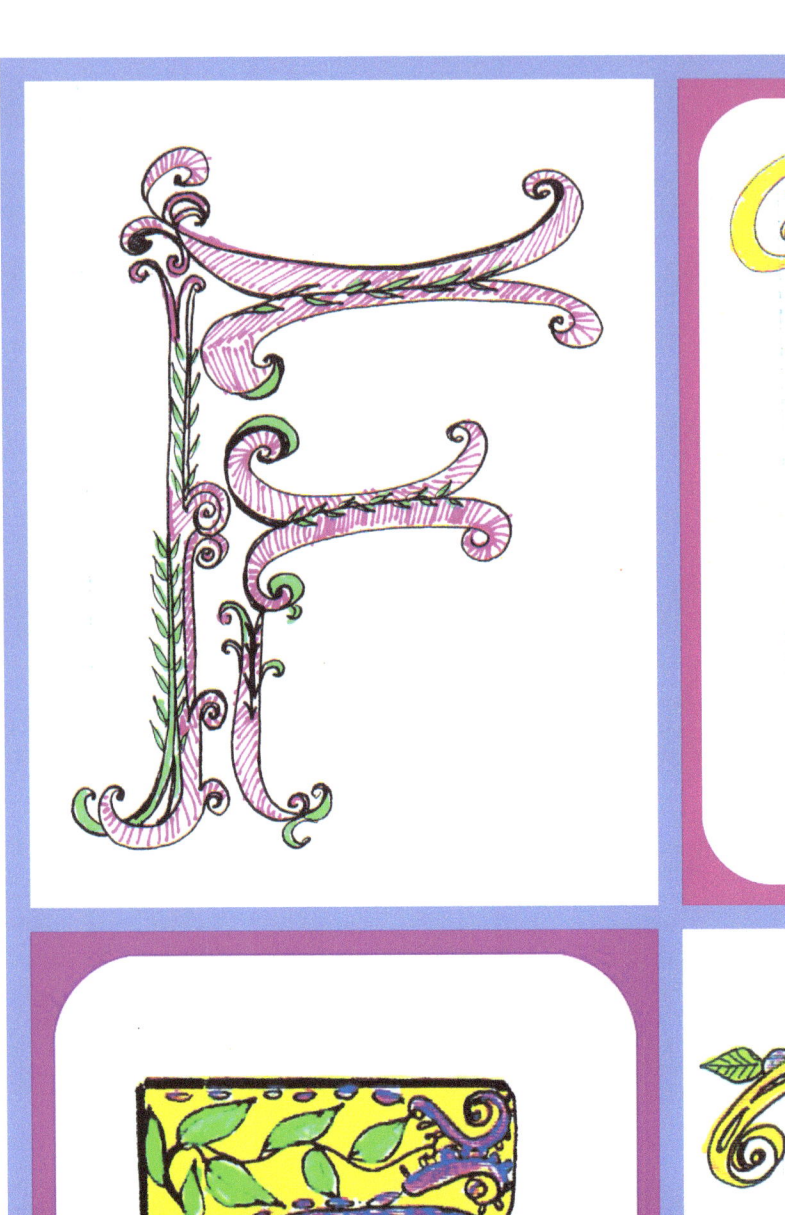

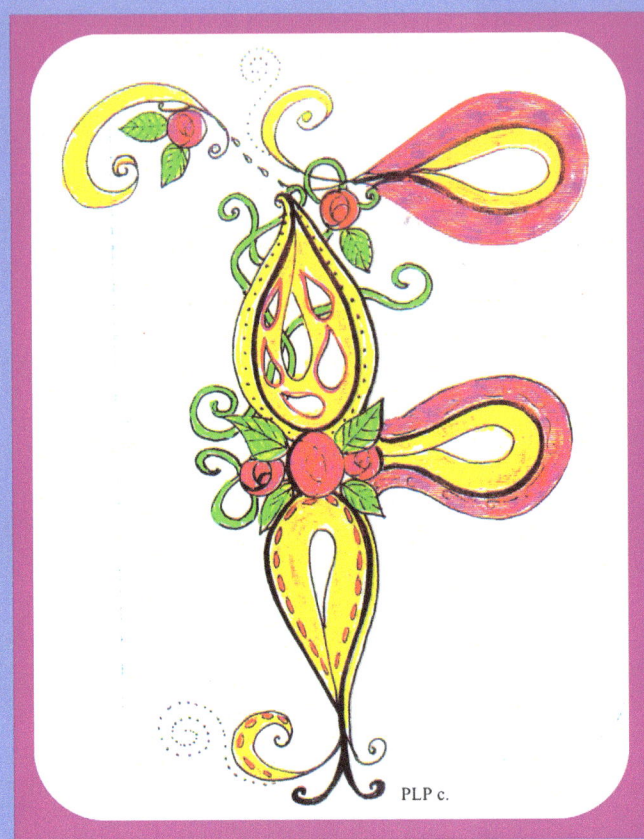

PLP c.

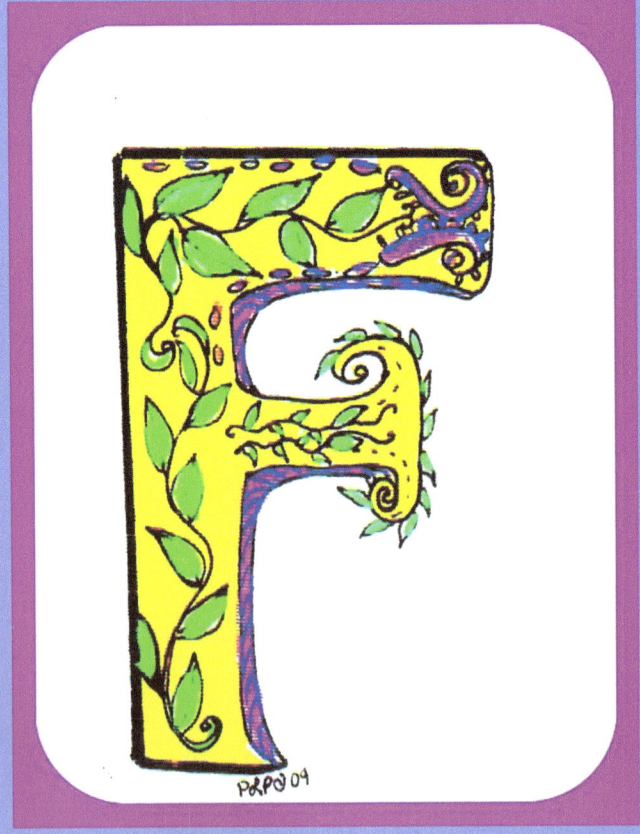

PLP 09

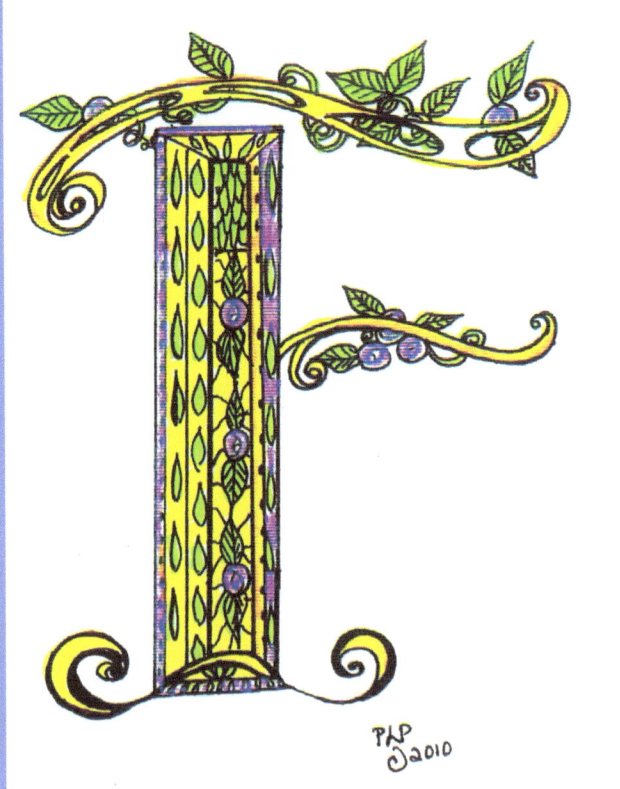

PLP 2010

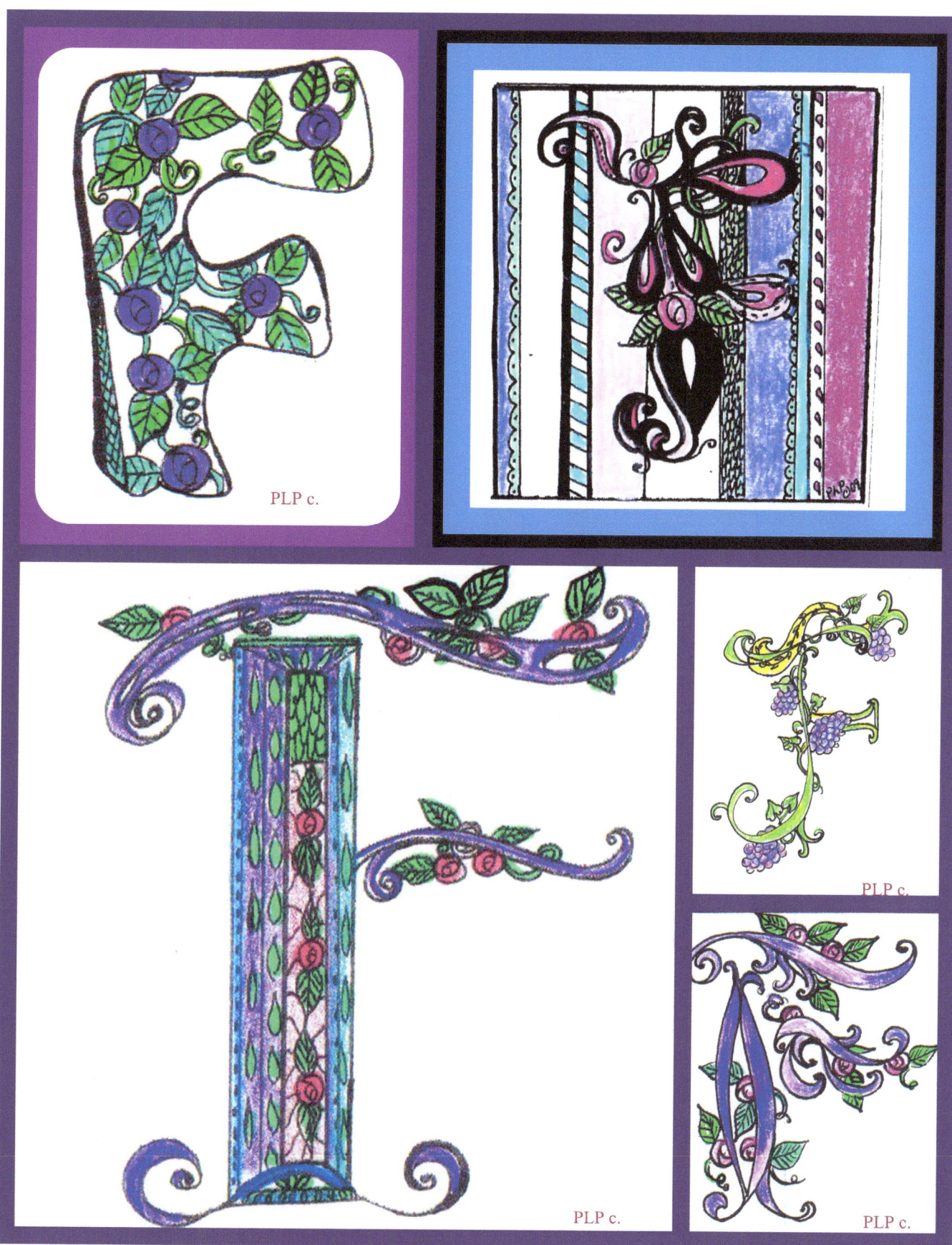

PLP c.

PLP c.

PLP c.

PLP c.

7

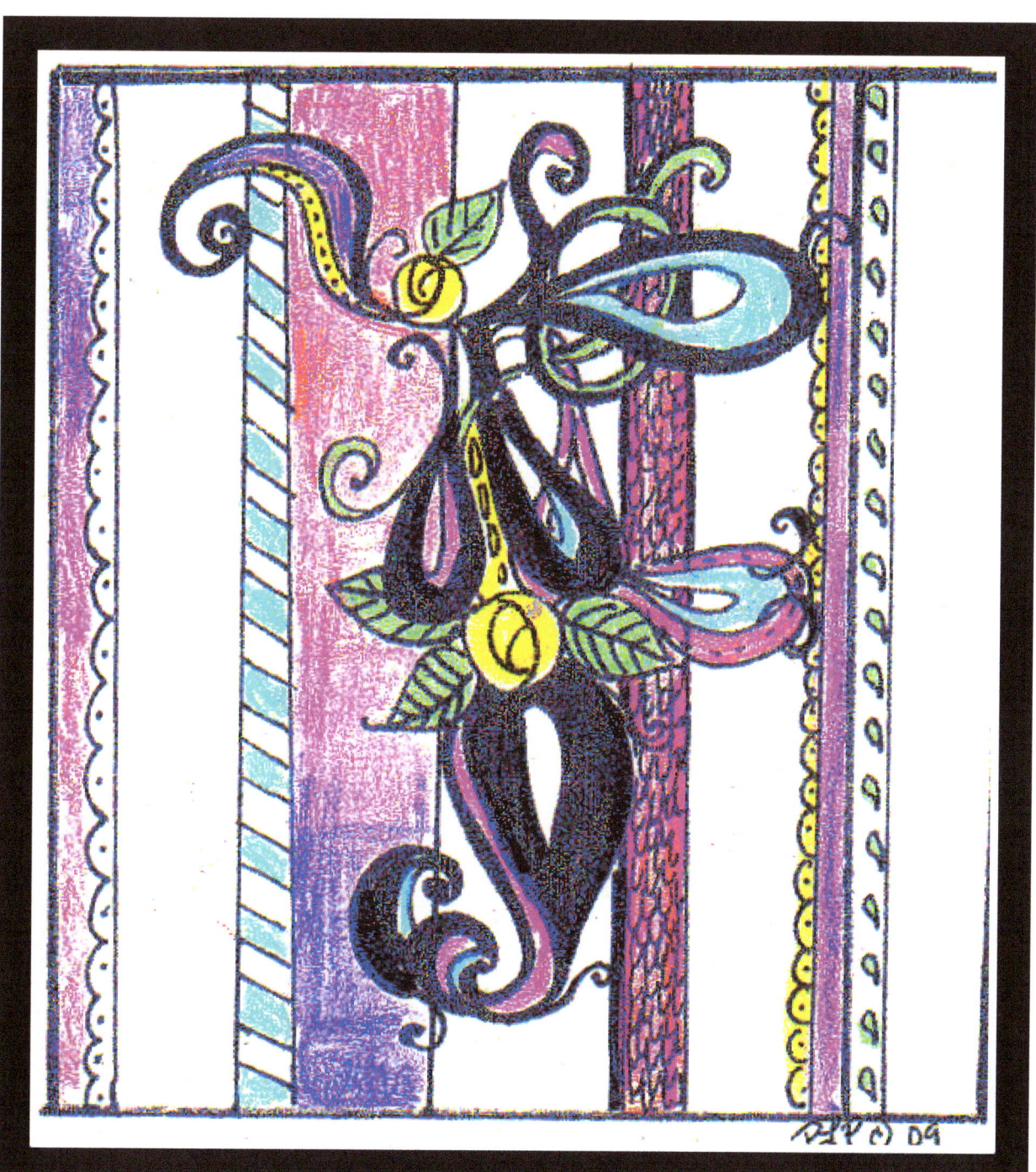

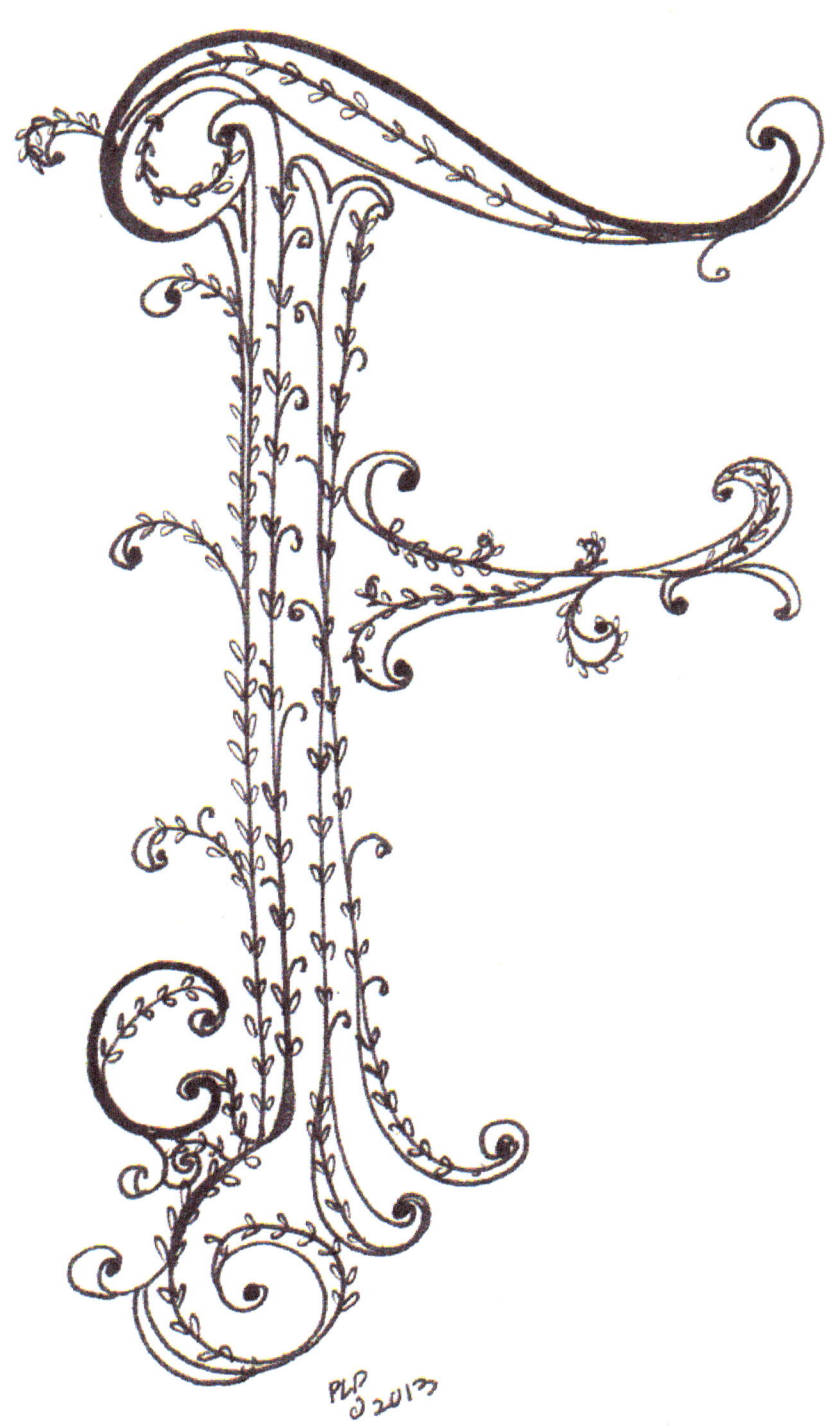

PLP
2013

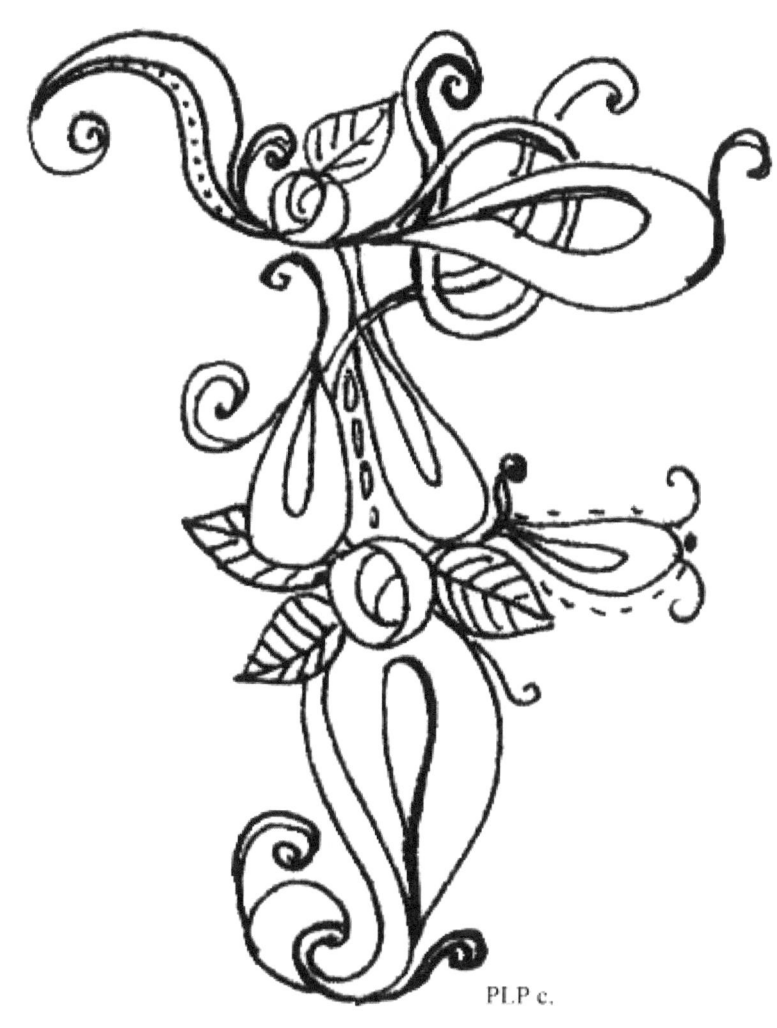

Pl.P c.

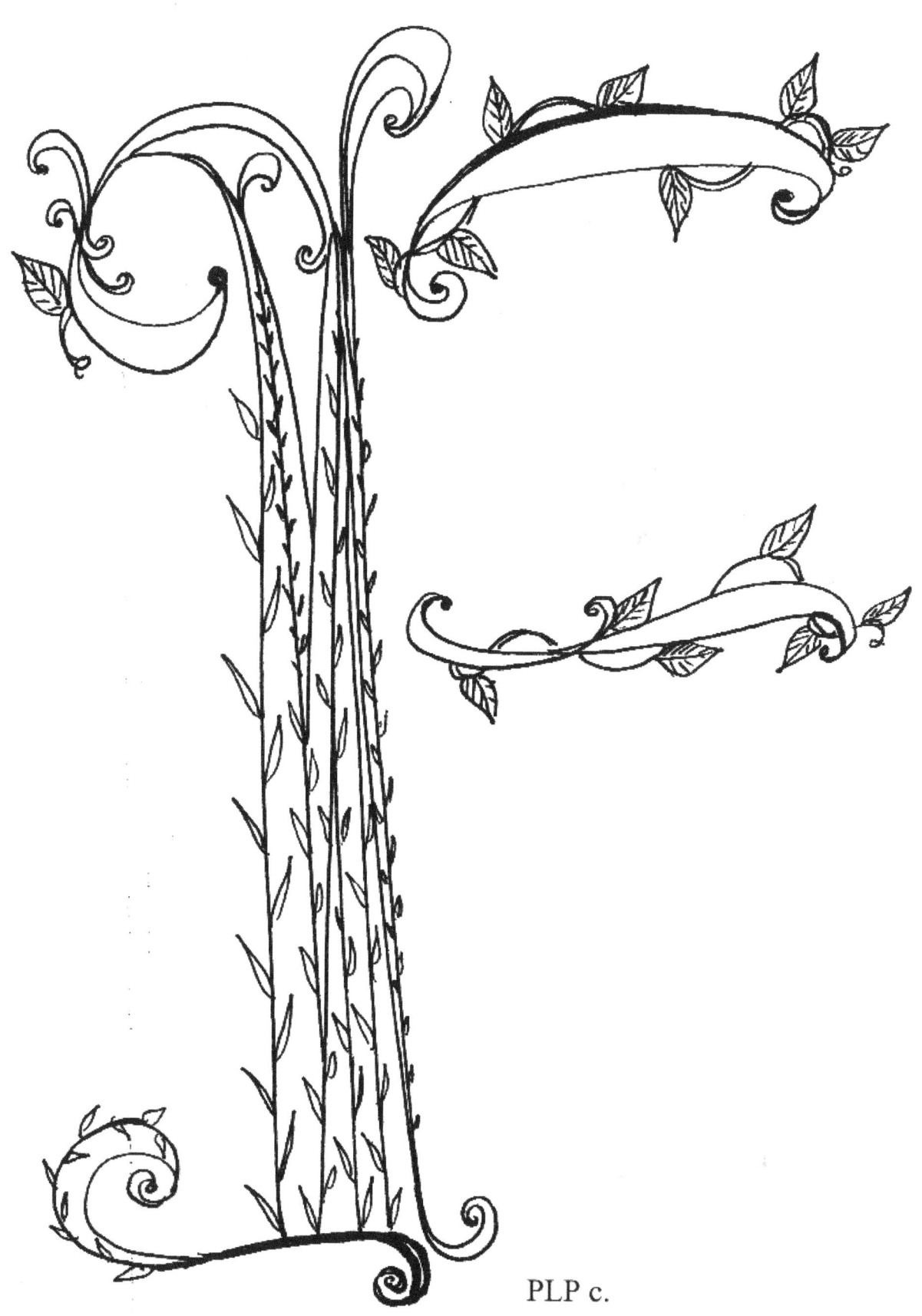

PLP c.

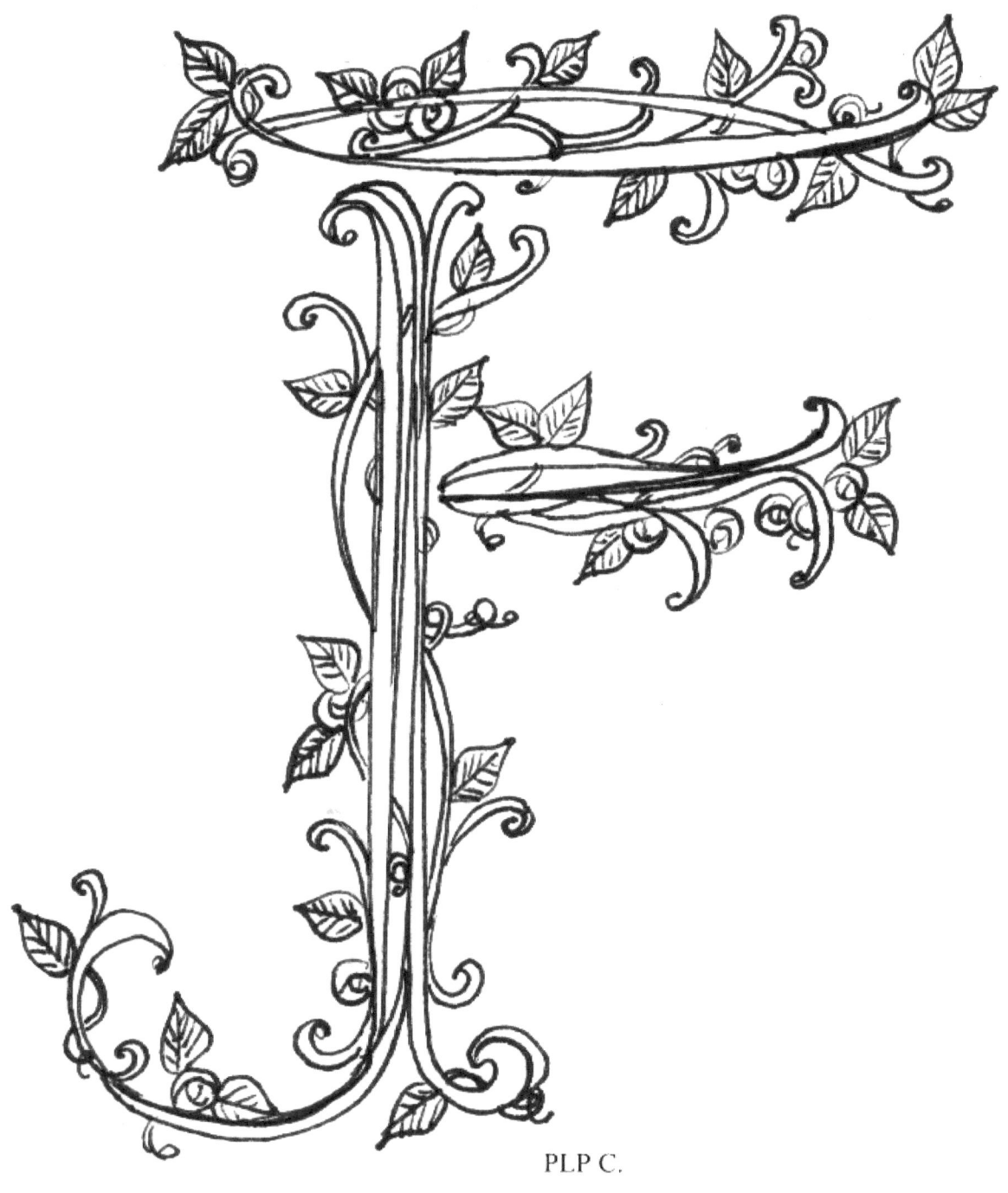

PLP C.

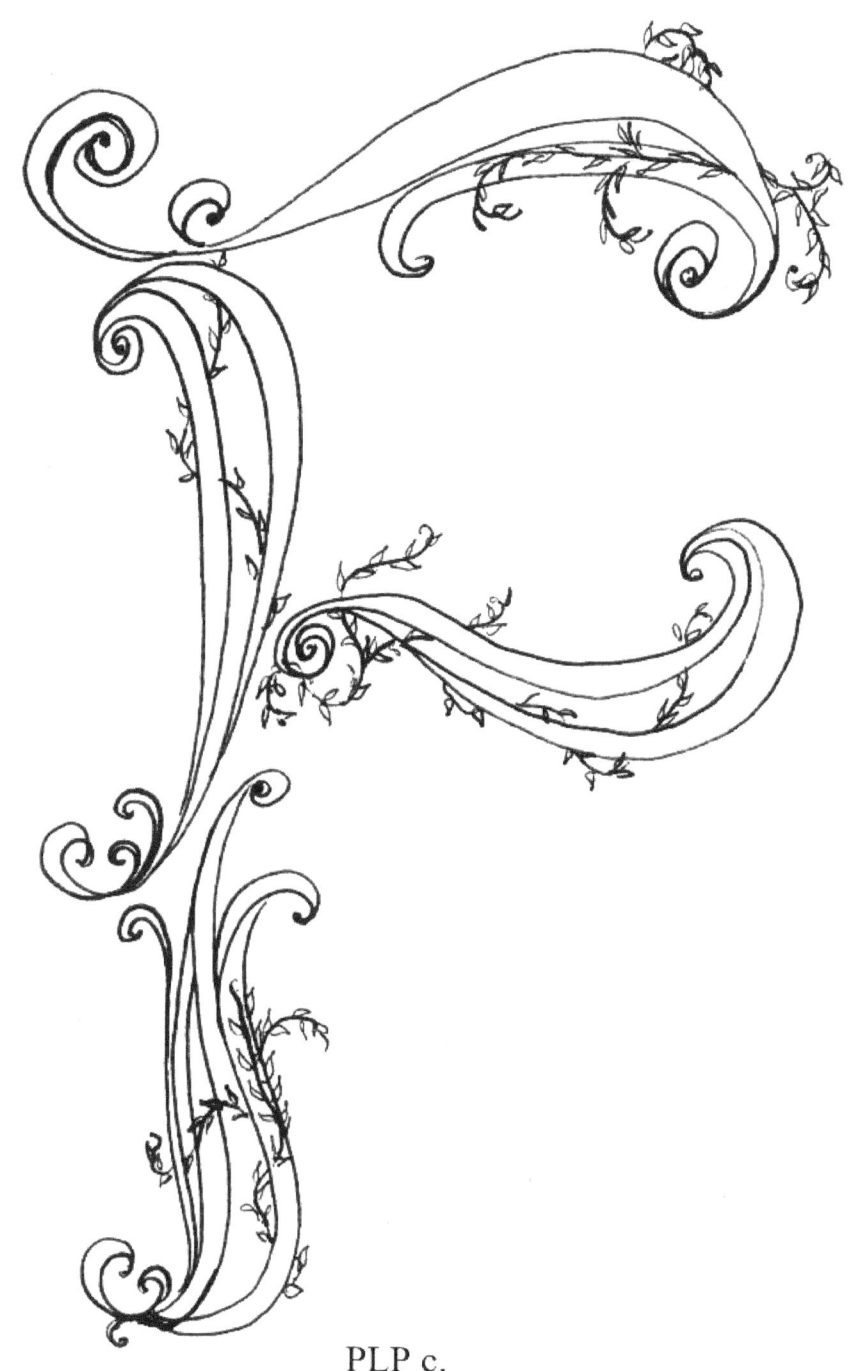

PLP c.

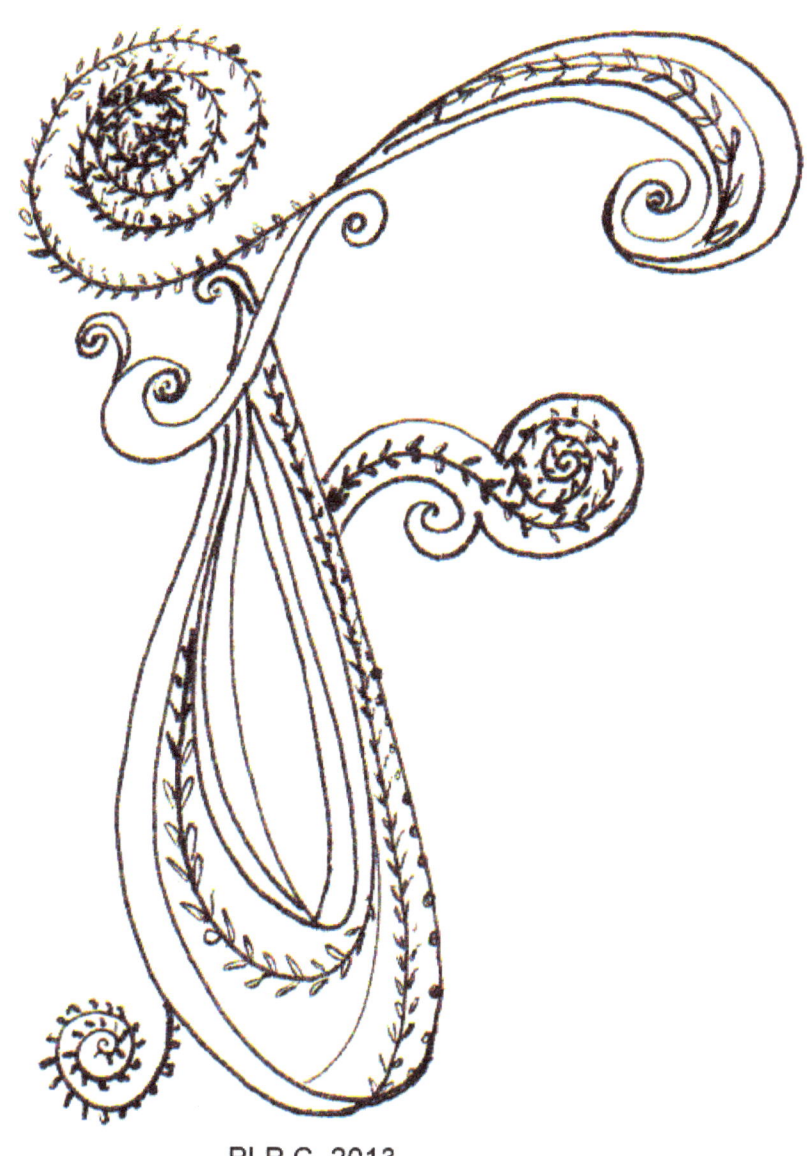

PLP C. 2013

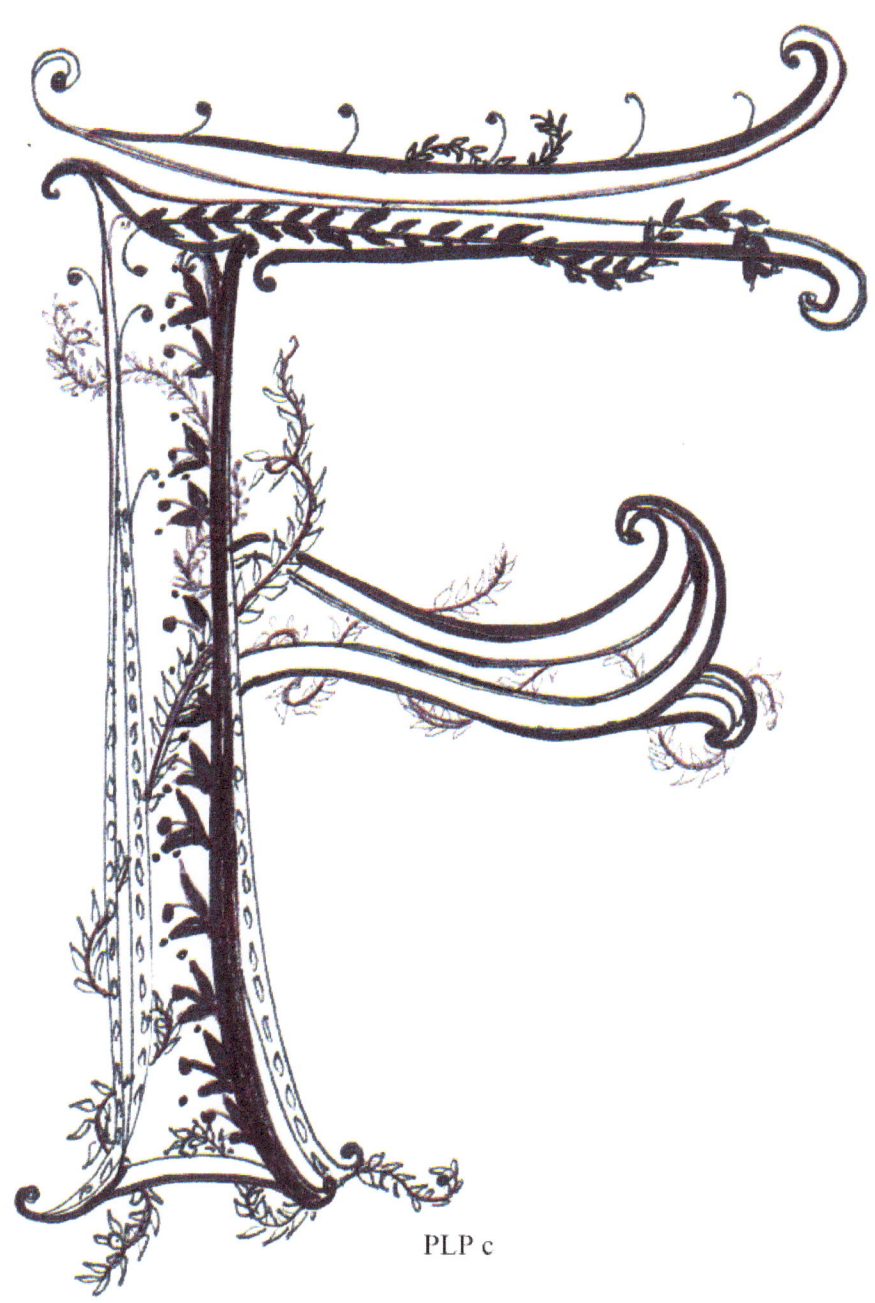

PLP c

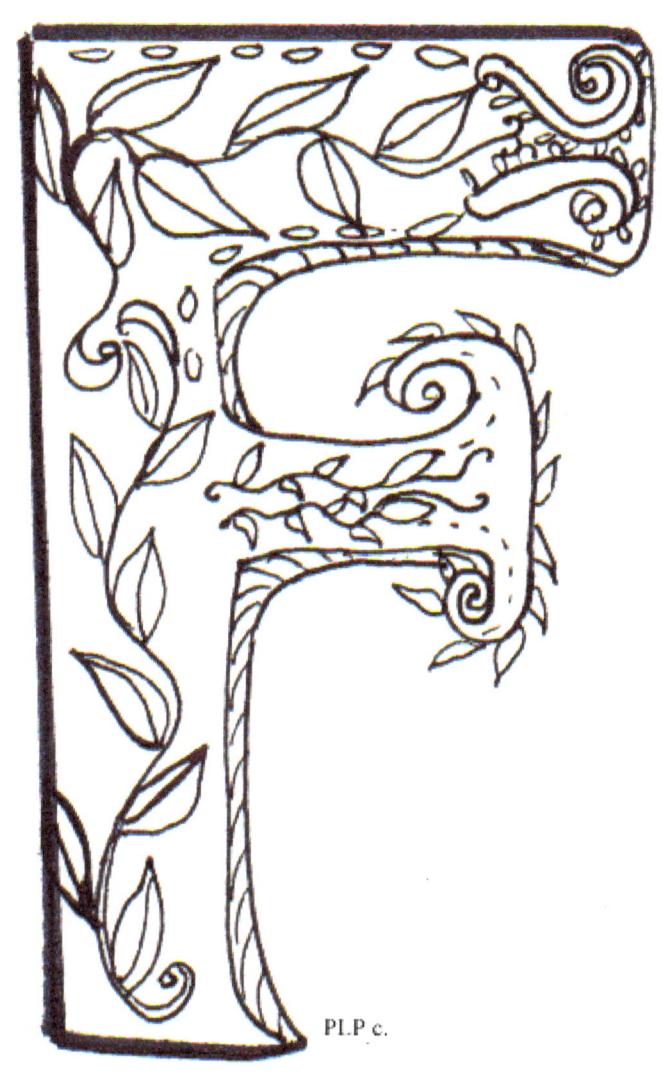

Pl.P c.

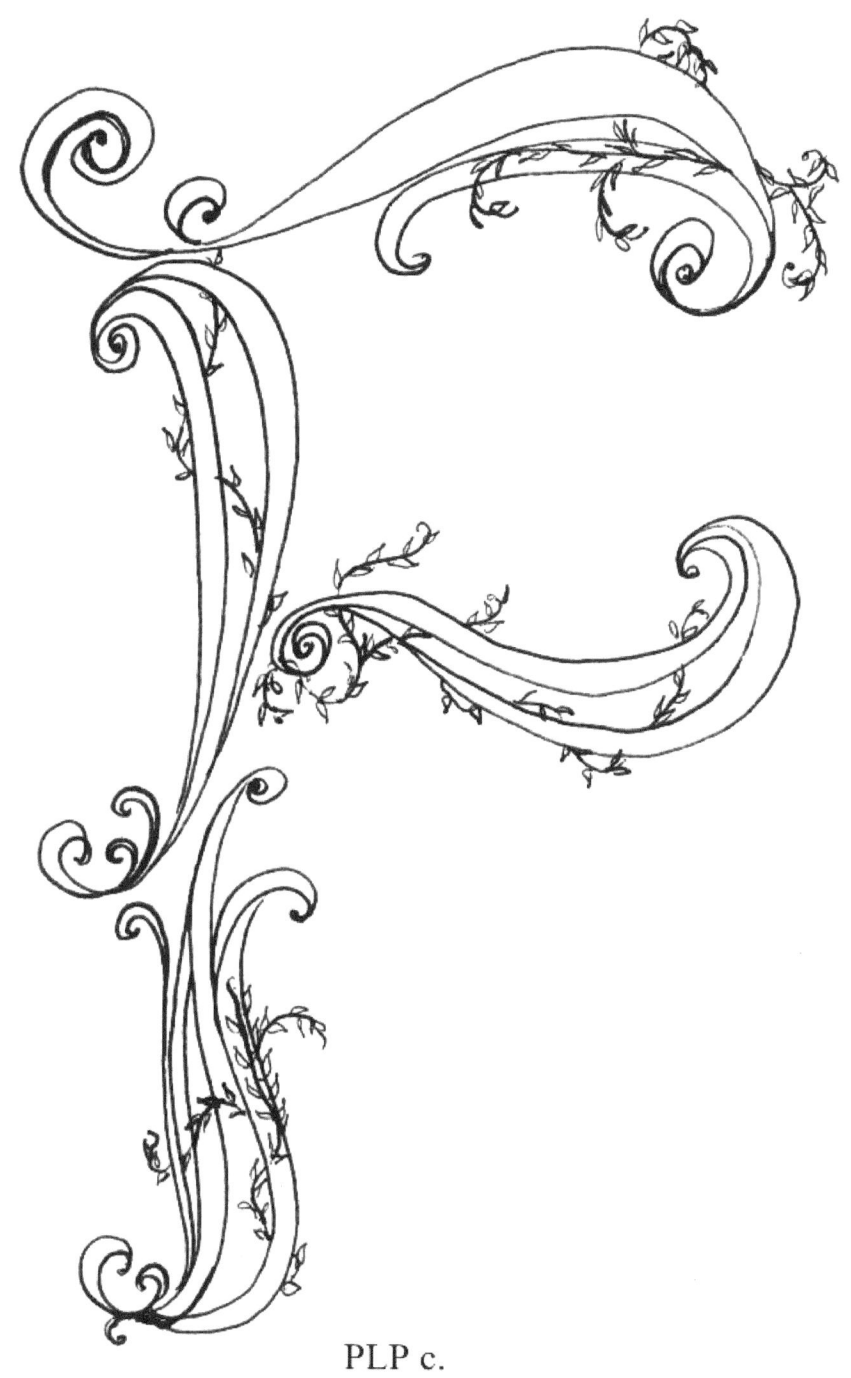

PLP c.

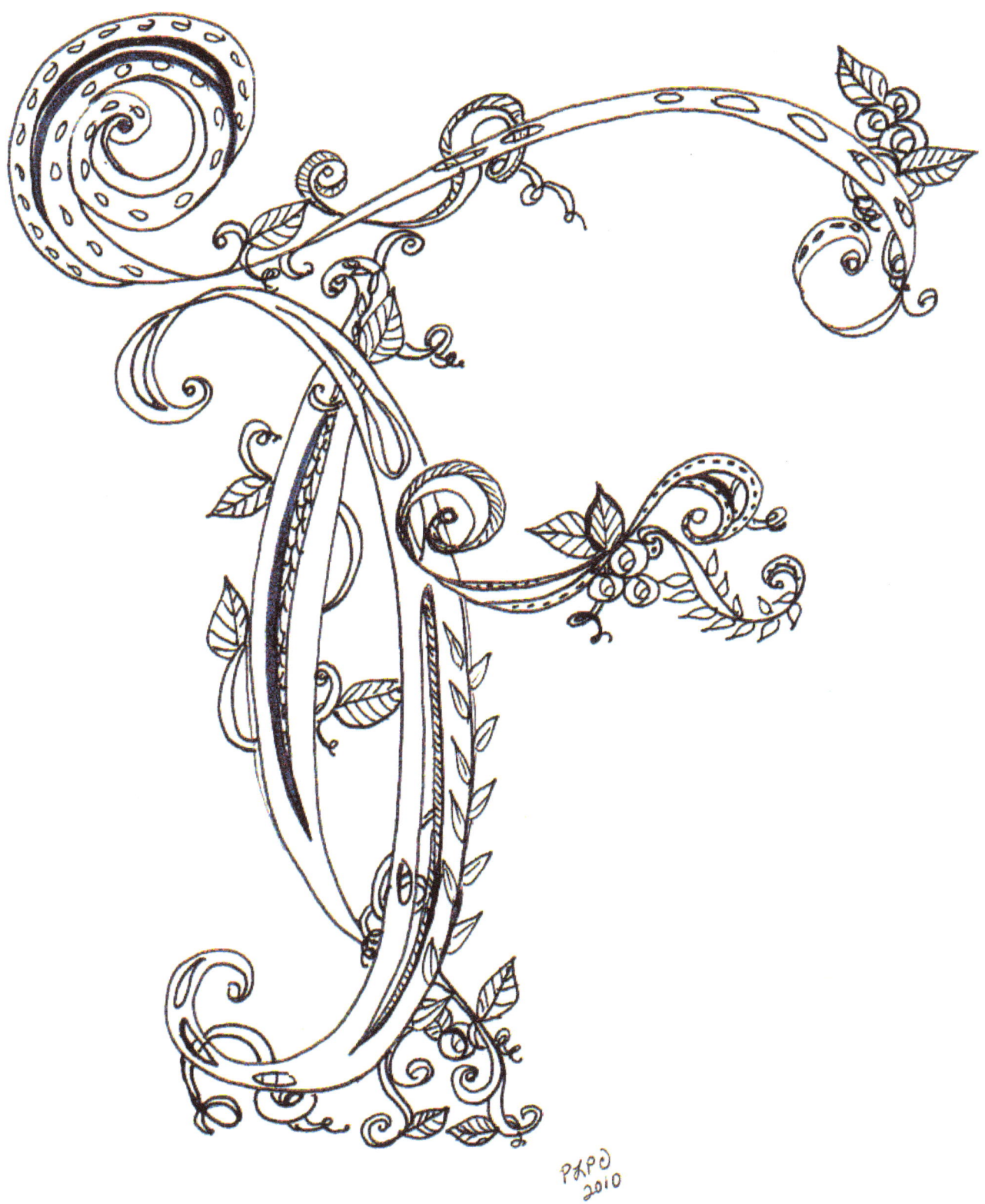

PLP c

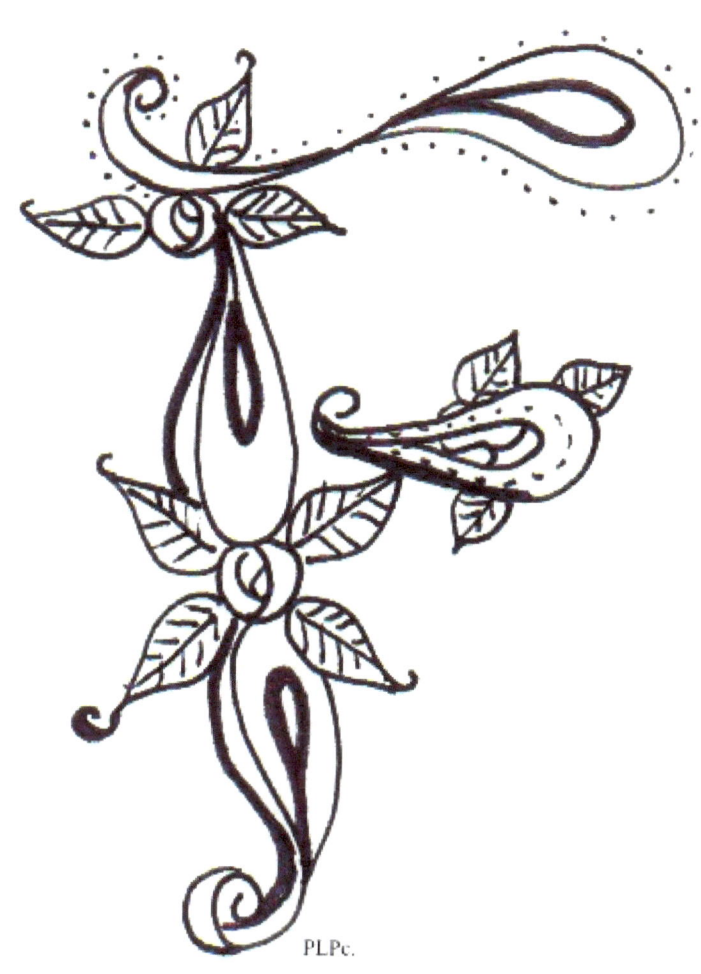

PLPc.

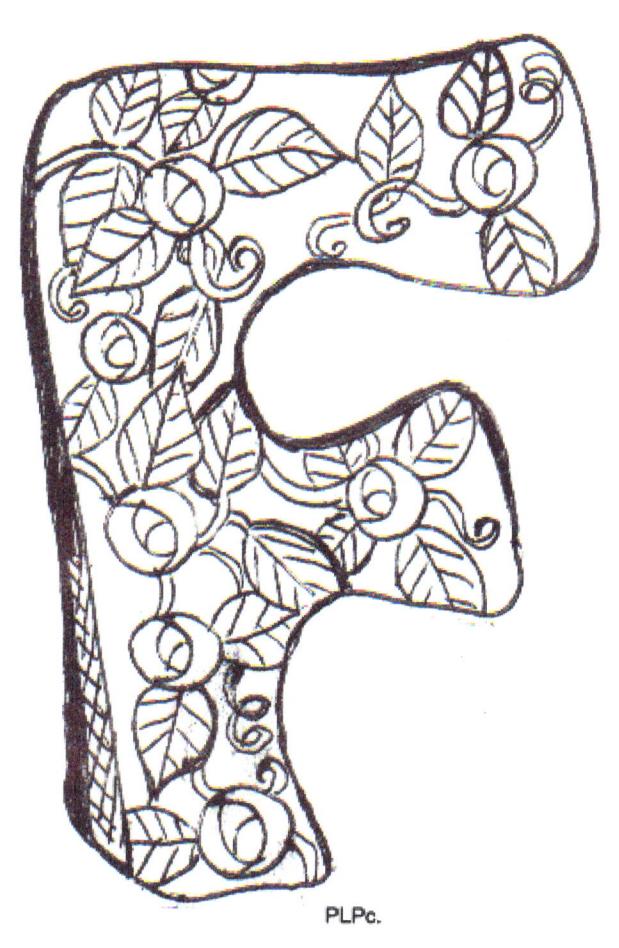

PLPc.

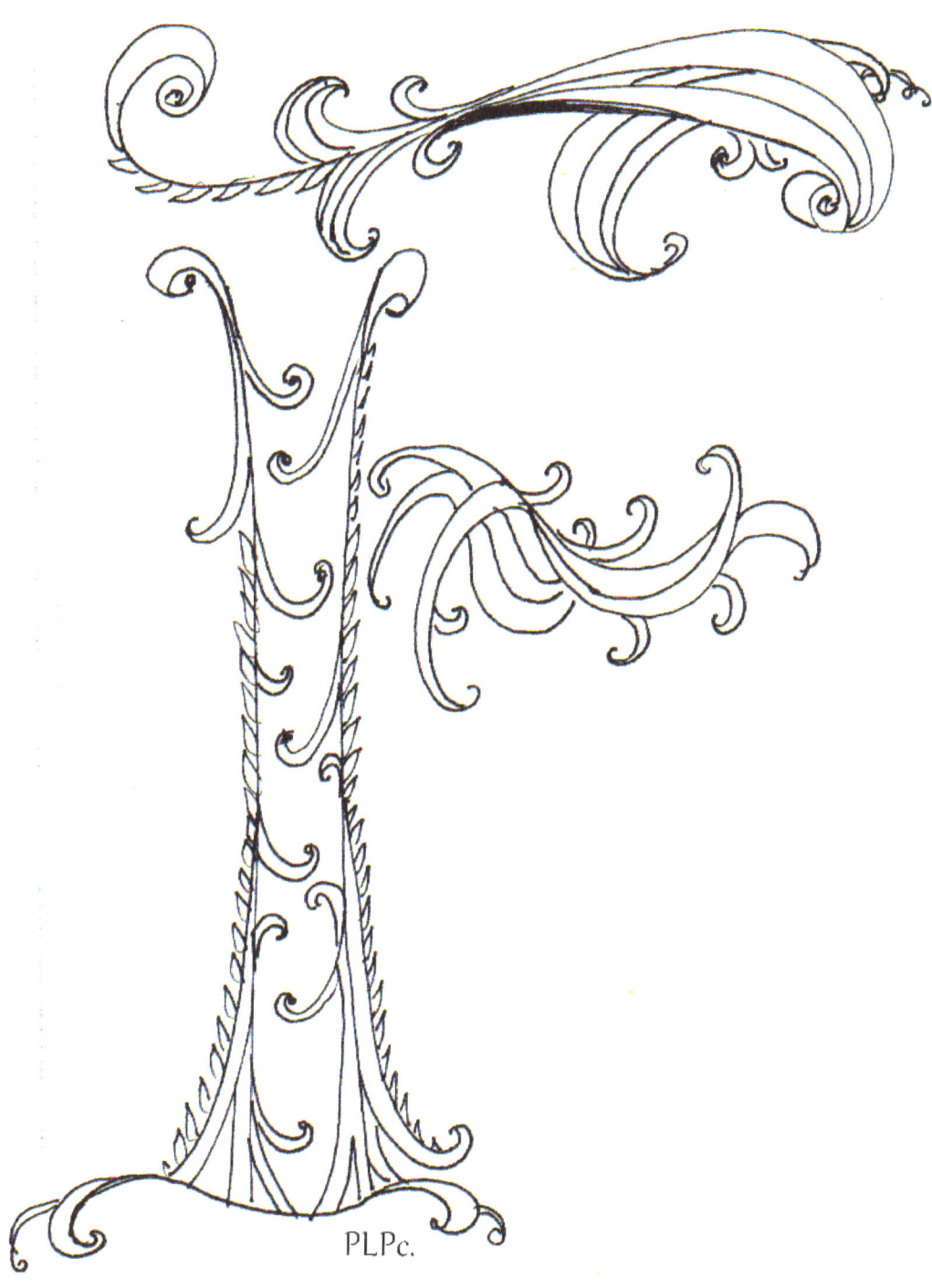

PLPc.

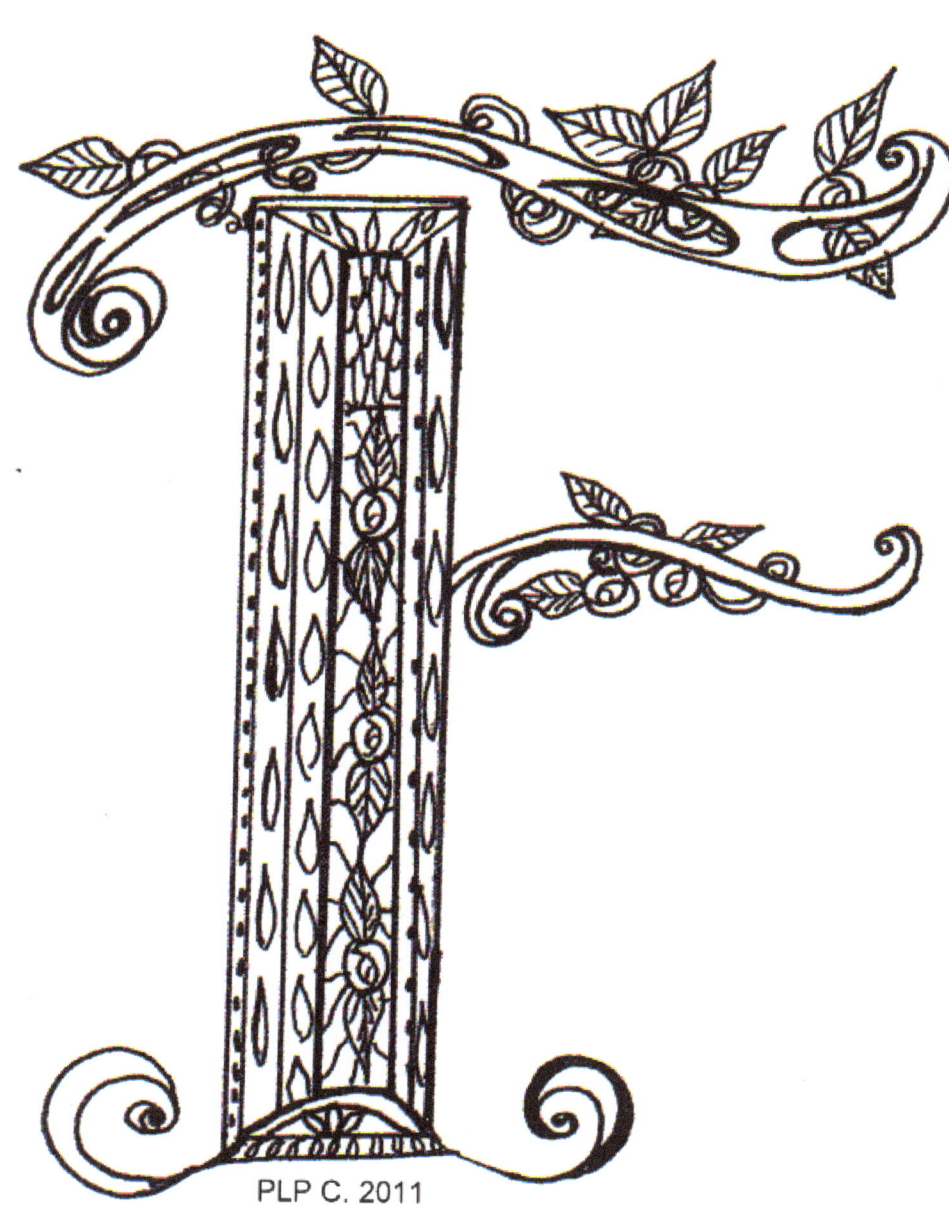

PLP C. 2011

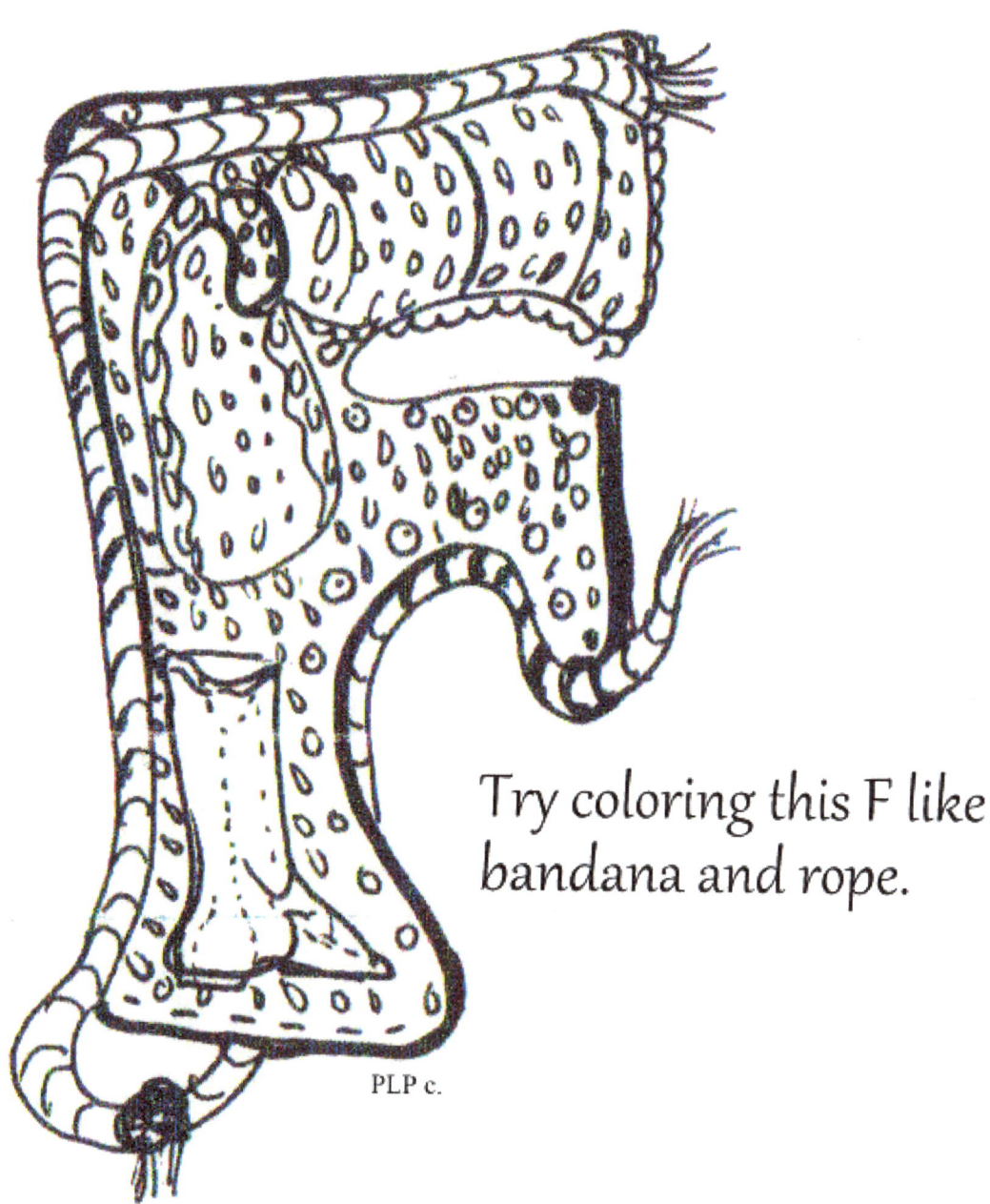

Try coloring this F like
bandana and rope.

PLP c.

41

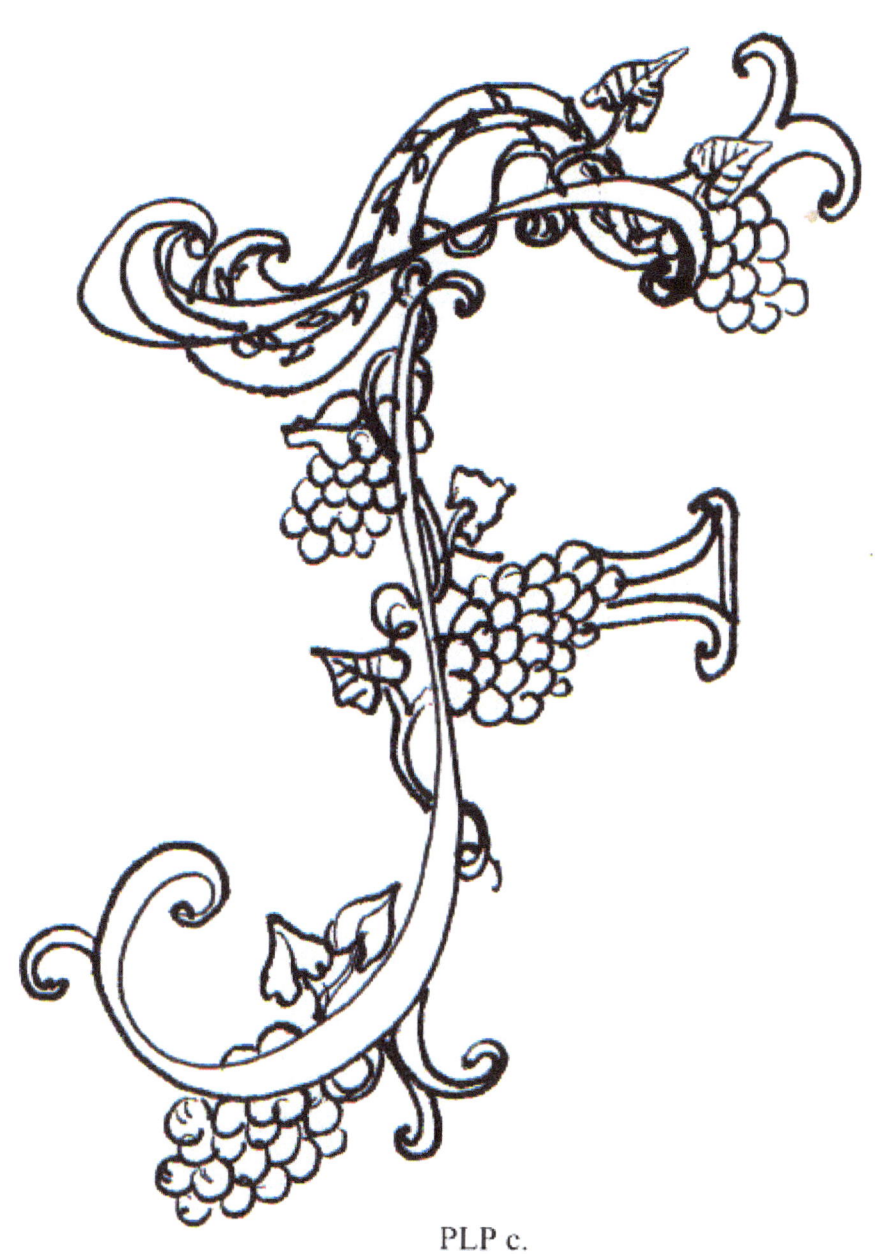

PLP c.

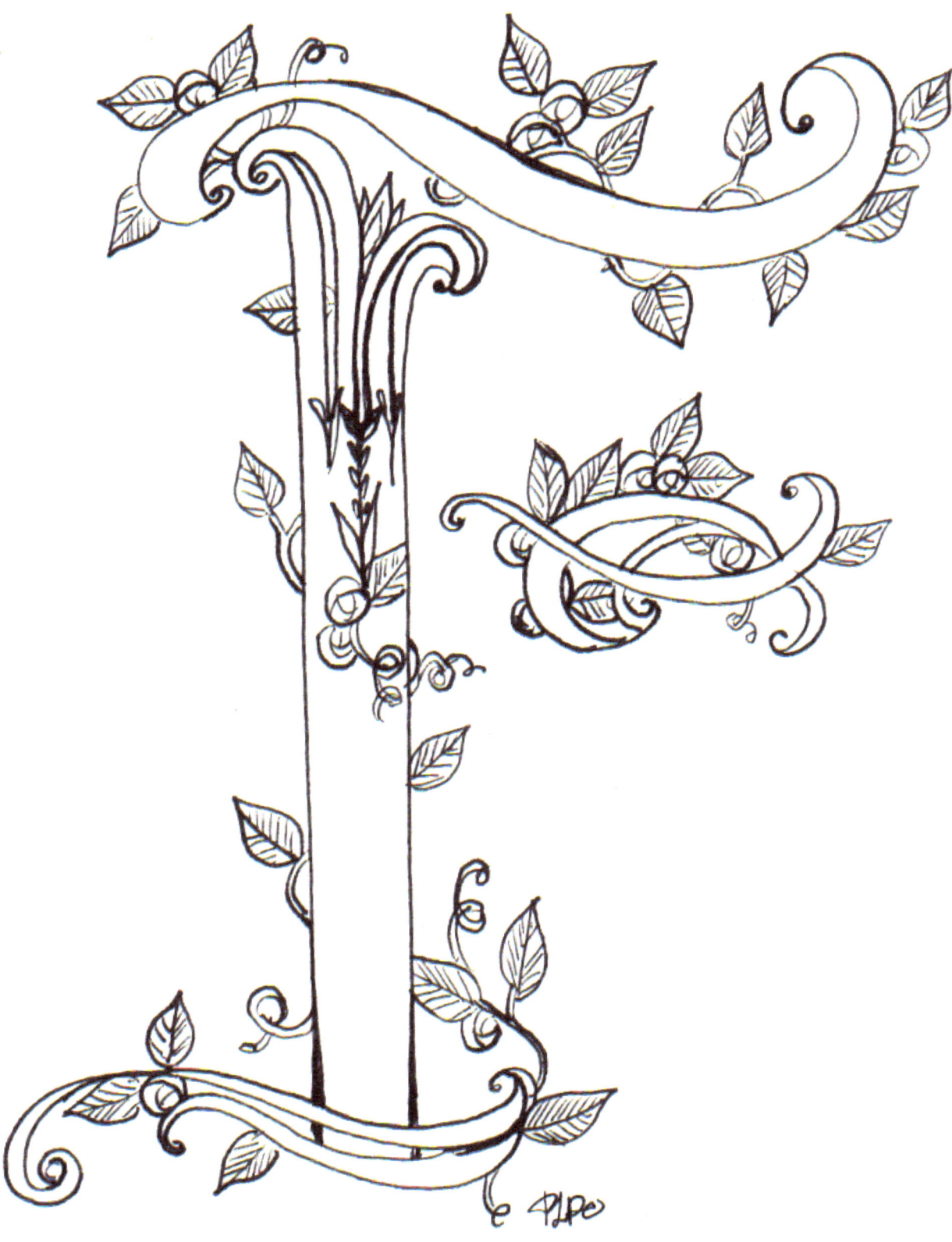

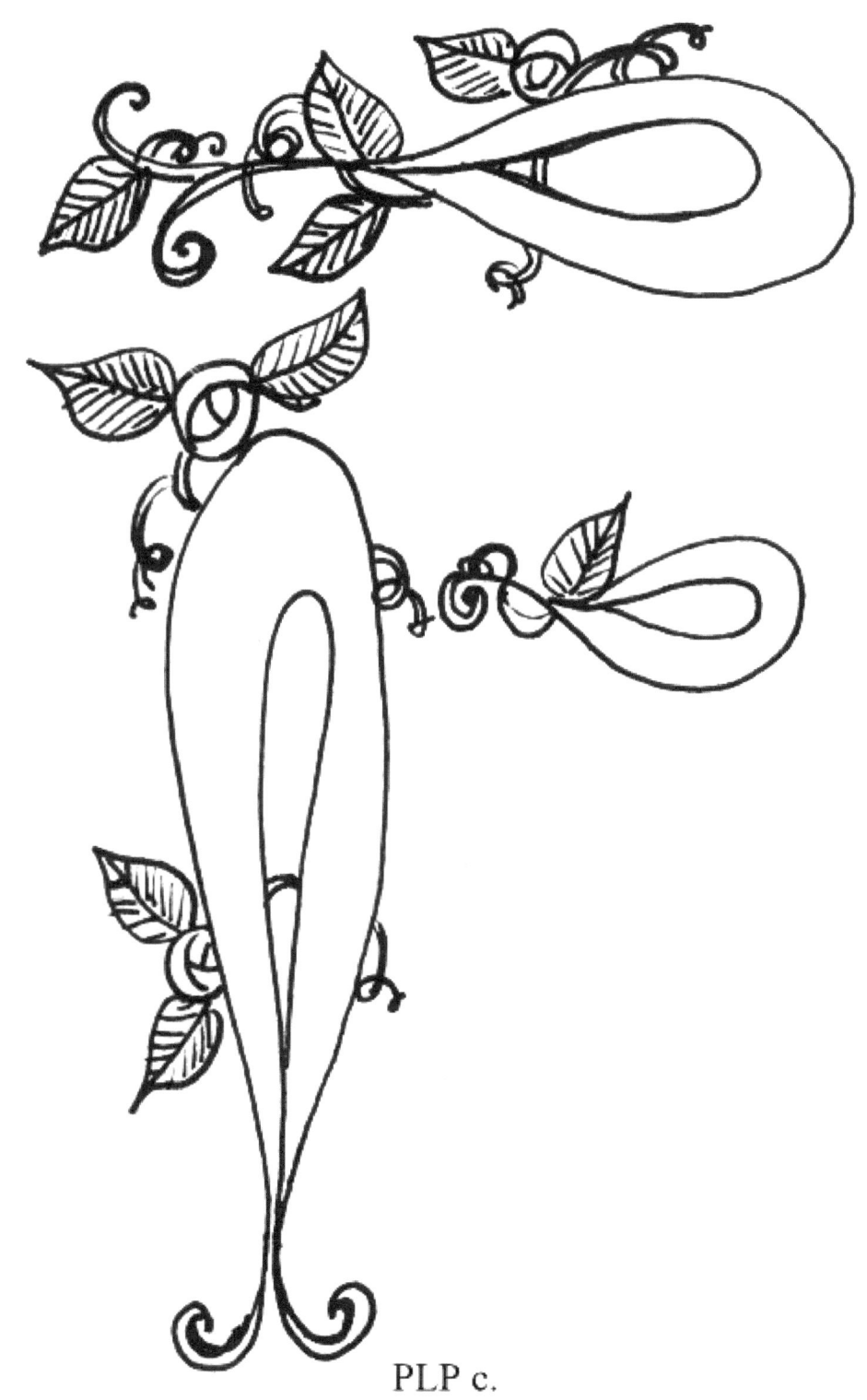

PLP c.

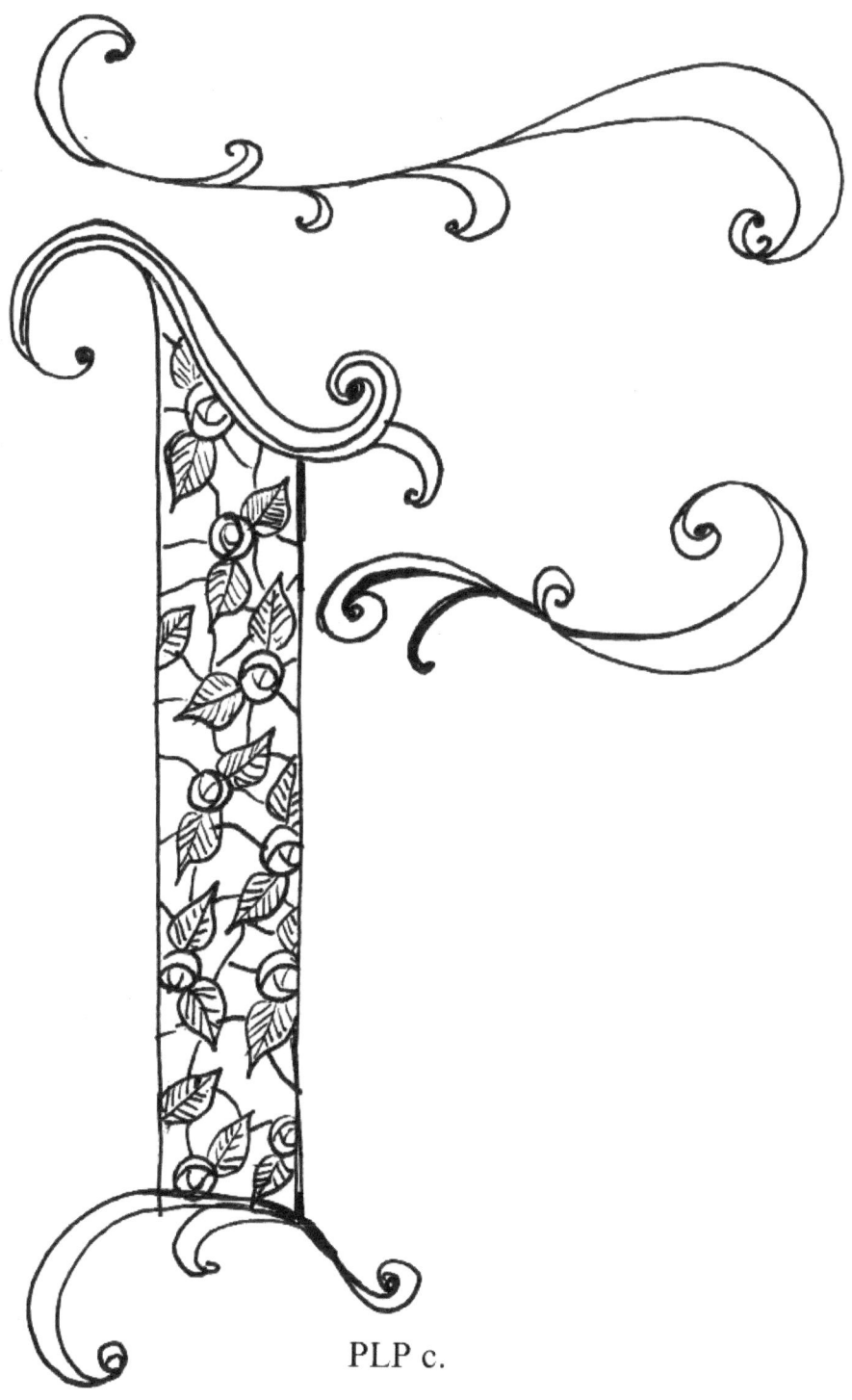

PLP c.

Did you see this F in this book?

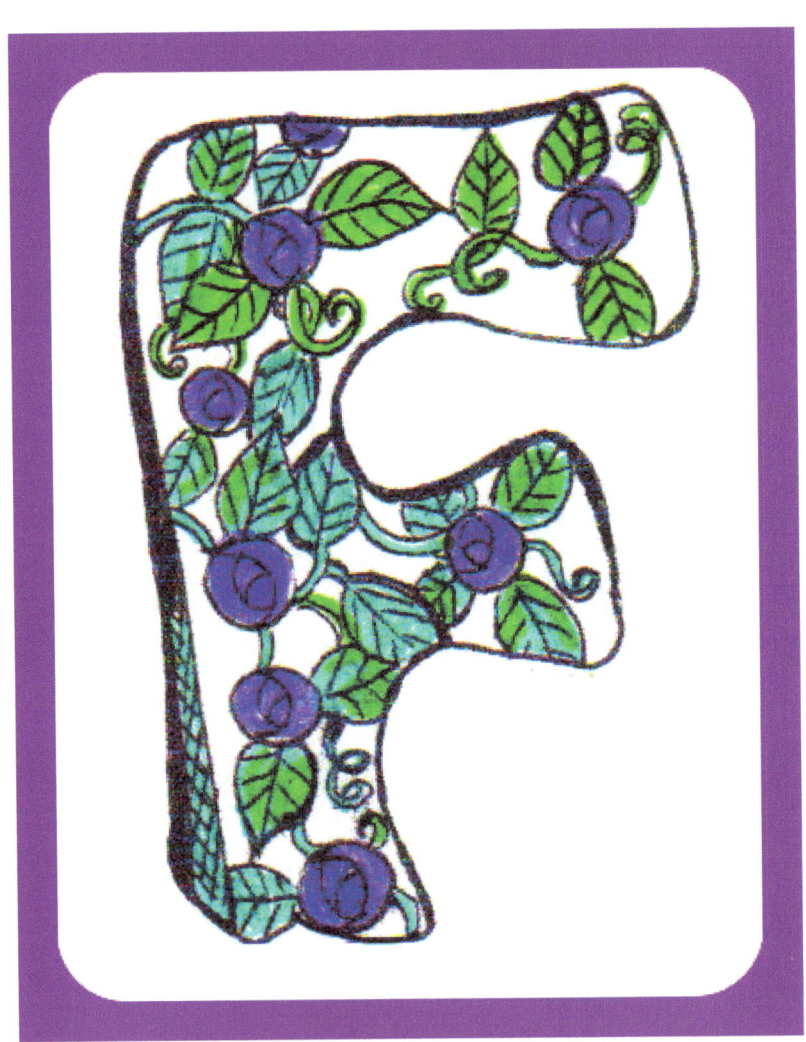

Fancy F letters can be used to start names or other words

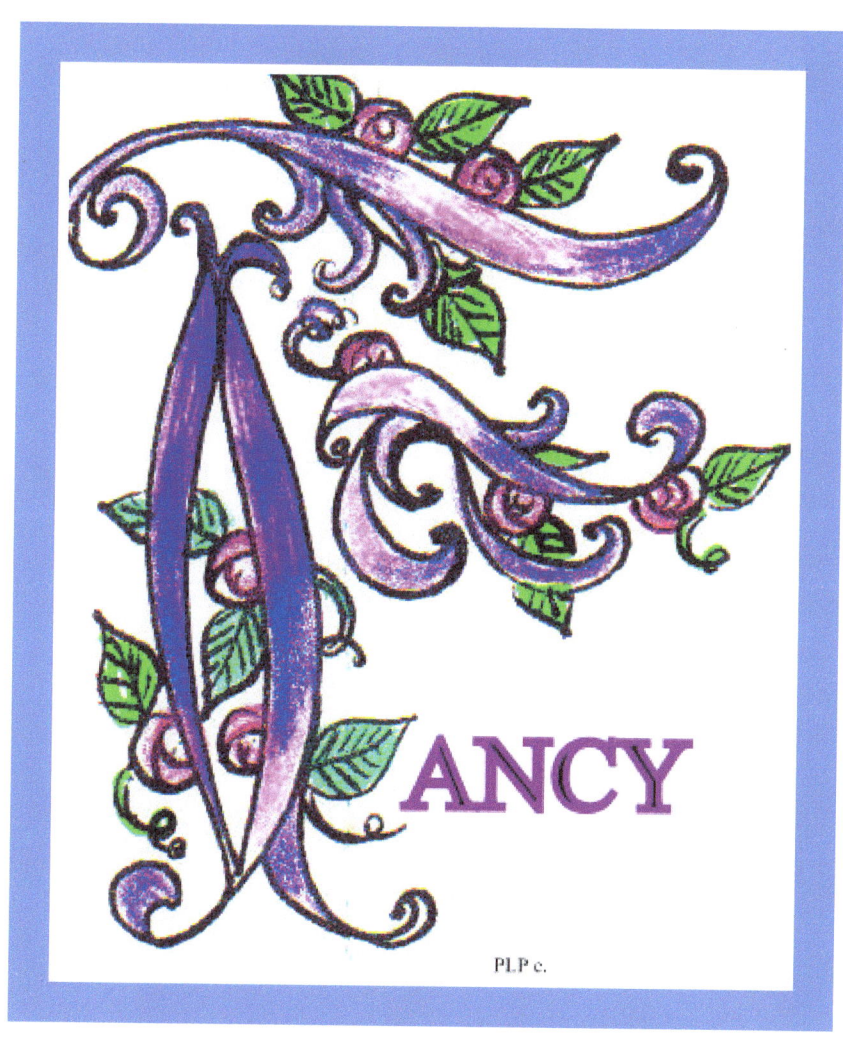

Thank you for visiting the letter Fs in this book. Visit the other Alphabet letters in my other books if you enjoyed coloring in this book.

Artist Peggy Louise Parrish